Day Trips to Eternity

Modern Spirituality Series

Creative Prayer
(Daily Readings with Metropolitan Anthony of Sourozh)

The Joy of Being
(Daily Readings with John Main)

Day Trips to Eternity

DAILY READINGS WITH LIONEL BLUE

Selected by
Daphne Richardson and Gordian Marshall

Darton, Longman and Todd
London

First published in 1987 by
Darton, Longman and Todd Ltd
89 Lillie Road, London SW6 1UD

© 1987 Lionel Blue

ISBN 0 232 51720 7

British Library Cataloguing in Publication Data

Blue, Lionel
  Day trips to eternity: daily readings
  with Lionel Blue.—(Modern spirituality).
  1. Spirituality
  I. Title   II. Richardson, Daphne
  III. Marshall, Gordian   IV. Series
  291.4   BV4501.2

ISBN 0–232–51720–7

Phototypeset by Input Typesetting Ltd
London SW19 8DR
Printed and bound in Great Britain by
Anchor Brendon Ltd, Tiptree, Essex

Contents

To Eva Berg,
my good companion

Introduction

I fell in love many years ago, when I was a student at Oxford. It happened just as the jukebox says: 'falling in love with love isn't just make-believe'. Because of this whiff of romance, I was rightly suspicious of it, and it took me years before I was sure it was not an illusion, a symptom of adolescence brought on by too much sublimation and too few outlets.

Spirituality, for me, is the consequence of that experience – trying to fathom its logic (or lack of it), its demands and lessons. Spirituality is not a word I use easily or comfortably, because I am not a see-through spirit. The Almighty did not make me that way, but an in-between creature, who is a little higher than the animals and a little lower than the angels. In practice, spirituality means learning to make something out of this mixture in me, not trying to wish it away.

I try to marry the demands of my soul and my body: my religious needs which come from on high, and the rates bill which comes through the letter-box; the demands of divinity and of my diet. (Prayer, after all, is not a substitute for exercise.) This is a traditional trait as well as a personal one, for the biblical tradition which Christians and Jews share never cared much for the immortality of the soul. It led instead to the resurrection of the body, messy as that is, theologically and practically. Unlike Greek, the Hebrew Bible has only one word for love, not two, and this has to serve whether love hits you in a vision or in bed. It is the reason why I suspect 'religious' voices on the radio, and why I do not trust truth on the higher slopes if there is no honesty on the lower ones.

By profession I am a fairly loyal member of a religious establishment, and do not deride it, because I know it has a similar nature to my own and a similar problem. At the beginning of my religious career I hoped it would be the communion of saints, and feared it might be a business. Well, like me, it is an in-between situation and has to be both in order to survive. Like most of the faithful, I cannot do with it as it is, but I cannot do without it either, so I need spirituality to make the holy compromises an in-between nature needs, compromises which are not just expedient ones. It took me a long time in prayer to realize that there can be good compromises, even holy ones, and these are my real work in life. Of course I find this in-between situation irritating, and at different times I have taken steps to resolve it – but they have never worked. If I try to give up the spirit, I become beastly, which beasts are not; and if I try to live just as a spirit, I become not saintly but silly.

Such knowledge and self-knowledge have been acquired painfully, but my 'spirituality' forced me to prefer reality to romance (it is not what I wanted, and that is why I trust it). I tried at the beginning of my love affair to take a short cut, and know God without knowing myself. But the kingdom of heaven is within you: all the best scriptures say so, or something similar, and if you try to know the former without the latter then your faith turns to fanaticism, banality or anorexia. Invoking the cosmos to avoid facing common, infantile hang-ups is out of proportion and absurd.

Although many Jews, like me, are uneasy about the word spirituality, if not the subject-matter it describes, there are in fact many schools and streams of it in Jewish history. The greatest and the grandest is the Kabbalah, whose central text is the book called Brightness or Zohar. It is the counterbalance to legal Judaism, and its anti-nomian backdoor. As a student I was fascinated by the questions it posed and wondered how the One became the many, how I can exist if God is totality and how the spark of divinity in me can be redirected to its source. Some of the problems were so daring, I took fright. Where is the hidden source of evil in the Godhead? For in the stark monotheism of Judaism rival devil figures are not plausible nor permitted.

I have never lost my interest in such preoccupations, but they are not relevant to my own life, as I have never had the will to wander further into the cosmologies, god maps and complex meditation systems of Kabbalah.

But there was another stream of spirituality which did not proceed from mighty mystics but from poor folk, mainly peasants, whose spirituality was concerned with different sorts of questions: how to suffer oppression without bitterness; how not to let poverty or pain sap the will to live; how to be a bit righteous and a bit holy in a concentration camp, in a slum or a suburb, or even in the media world of Hollywood or Broadway. Such spirituality exists among all religious people (and in many who do not know they are) and it was especially rich among the poor Jews of Eastern Europe, from which my own family came.

Saints have never played the same role among Jews as among Christians. The word 'saint' itself (like 'spirituality') does not have a comfortable feel when applied to individuals. In the Bible it is used only of God or, very occasionally, the entire people – never of a person, even if he is Moses. The Talmud, too, is built up out of thousands of opinions. Of those who held them, we know little; of many of them we know nothing, not even their names (only, in fact, the opinions). In modern times, the book of the holocaust – its 'scripture', so to speak – was not written by a rabbi, but by Anne Frank, an ordinary adolescent who kept her integrity in an extraordinary situation.

Their way of spirituality is expressed not in ecstatic or esoteric treatises but in stories, jokes, sayings, graffiti and diaries. They arise out of the struggles in numerous little people's lives, and for me they have the ring of relevance and truth.

My generation lives in the shadow of the holocaust, and my own spirituality has to cope with the questions it left behind. They are not refined questions but the crude ones ordinary people ask, and since there are no sleight-of-hand answers to them, spirituality means living with them and exploring them – not solving them.

The first is, where can we locate God in the horror of it? He cannot be identified with the religious institutions which (apart from special individuals) behaved not much better or worse than their secular counterparts. (This is a discomforting fact, but true spirituality means accepting uncomfortable truths, as Teresa of Avila says and many rabbis too.)

The second is that so many pleas and prayers must have been said, on the journey to the concentration camps, which were never answered in any way most of us can understand. So why pray? Or, what should we be praying for? Perhaps miracles occur here and there, but in our time they did not seem to occur where they were wanted or needed. For too many, the waters of the Red Sea did not part.

But life goes on, as ordinary people know, and it cannot be lived without a practical spirituality, even if the theoretical questions have to gather dust in the 'unanswered' file. We cannot do justice to ordinary life without invoking eternity.

It is this practical spirituality which does not descend from the heights, but is pieced together from below, which now brings together Christians, Jews, people of all religions and of none, and of all classes. It is trusted because it speaks of situations people can recognize and of a spirituality whose insights can be verified for truth and relevance. Their acceptance does not depend on repetition, which is the usual way people convince themselves of things they are not sure they believe.

It also avoids the trap of a romantic guruism, inflated by the media, which can make morons of many of its own devotees. The truth is complex and each of us has a bit of it. In daily life we make a composite guru out of such bits, and redeem each other. It is the do-it-yourself, democratic spirituality of the radio and television.

It does not need a hot-house atmosphere for it to thrive. Its lessons can be learnt in bus queues and taught on transistors. You do not have to be on your knees or in any formal pose to receive it. You can meditate the truths of radio religion while soaking in a bath or covered in cold cream or shaving soap. These truths are the same, whether you come to them searching for happiness or holiness, piety or pleasure. They carry no religious labels, so even secularists are not suspicious of them.

I first began to understand this common way to God when I studied the Talmud at my seminary and wondered what use (if any) such learning would ever be to me later. Who would ask me whether you could take a book upstairs on a festival, or how you could carry a handkerchief on the Sabbath? Well, hardly anybody has asked, but my lessons were not wasted, because they taught me that God is in the trivial as well as in the grandiose; and, in any case, who knows what is trivial or grandiose in the eyes of eternity, and which will be preferred?

People find by ordinary experience that even if they want to be materialists, they cannot be, because the material world does not work that way. It seems full of promise, but somehow the actual promises are not kept. Take holidays, for example: the ordinary package ones. The brochures do not lie (in my experience), yet people come home disappointed. Yes, they had a twin-bedded room, with PB, SV, B/Sh and three (three-course) meals a day. So their comfort problem was solved. But happiness did not come along as an automatic extra, as they had hoped and expected. When they puzzle it out, they realize that happiness is not an object but a state of mind – usually acquired by giving, not receiving. To enjoy ourselves we need to give some joy to others. Otherwise, it is another example of the old spiritual conundrum, 'what is the sound of the hand-clapping?'

Also, the experience of another dimension, of eternity, of the life of the world to come is not unusual. It is quite a common one, though many people do not know how to recognize it or use it, because they have not been trained to, and they throw away their experience of it. Though the unseen gravity of that other dimension or world cannot be seen, its effects are obvious and commonplace. It pulls people out of their comfortable seats on crowded trains and makes them offer these seats to others. It draws them to acts of self-sacrifice and generosity which astonish no one more than themselves. It makes heroes and martyrs of unremarkable people. There are few who have never felt it.

There are few also who do not pray sometime, somewhere. What they pray for, they probably do not get, and they are not surprised. Commonsense people know the universe is unlikely to change its course to suit their convenience. After all, if it did not happen in the concentration camps, why should it happen for more trivial predicaments? But ordinary people are not fools and they carry on praying, because something in them and in their prayers changes with them as they pray. The purification process is starting to work in them. They might not know the theological terms to describe it, but they feel it. They also know that though security is not on offer (whatever churches or synagogues say), they can in practice gain courage through prayer, which helps them over hurdles they could not otherwise cope with.

There are many religious recipes on offer, so consumers have understandably become cautious about which to invest their lives in. Like me, most rely on a scripture (or two) which has been handed down, and also on their own personal scripture, which they have puzzled out for themselves on park benches, in hospital waiting-rooms and on their bed awake and alone in the middle of the night (like the unknown psalmist, who might have been David, or some anonym).

But spirituality is not simply a private matter; it is a public one. For me this is obvious. Being a rabbi, I am concerned with other people's spirituality as well as my own. I am not paid to pursue my own path to paradise, but to educate, coax, scold and entertain a community so that they can have a taste of paradise on earth, if such is possible. It is also obvious to non-professional religious peoples as well. The problems of the third world are known, even if we do not know how to solve them. We think they are material (and many of them are), such as poverty, hunger and land reform. But the affluent, insecure West has its needs too, and they are boredom, anxiety, addiction and loss of purpose. They are our counter parts to the needs of the third world. But they are spiritual and therefore just as difficult to answer.

Sooner or later, even if the economics are successful, the way of affluence peters out. One car is necessary, two are a convenience, three are a luxury, but four show a lack of imagination. When people search for pleasure in a hedonist society, the path to it boomerangs. It leads them back to themselves – not to what they have, but to what they are. I am not whining about modern comforts, of which I have been and am a beneficiary, I am simply pointing out that affluence, hedonism and consumerism need spirituality to help them deliver their goods, and the happiness they promise. The learning is two-way. The secular world has things to teach as well as to learn. Religion has in the past been fuzzy, confusing history, folklore and mythology. The truth can be taught in many ways, but modern people are more used to the language of semi-science. I doubt if spirituality can ever achieve the precision of, say, an aircraft engine, but it must try. Marx and Freud, for example, are not names which religious people find sympathetic – understandably so. But 'the truth shall make you free' (as I have quoted earlier) and there are truths in both, which all societies have had to accept. (If it is any comfort, Freud can be more unpopular among Marxists than among believers.) The society around us conditions us as Marx taught, and we have to know ourselves as we seek to know God, for the kingdom of heaven is within us.

Secular fashions also condition our spirituality, although we are not conscious of them, for faith does not exempt us from the society which creates them and of which we are a part, willy-nilly. In the 1950s and 1960s young people tried to bypass the world with its economic and political huckstering. They sought spirituality in far-off places. But because they did not want to 'work at' the world, the world hit back and hijacked their search for saintliness. Business empires were built out of spiritual yearning, and much money was made. They tried to get a trip to heaven but got taken for a ride.

Now that the hippies are history, and the flower-power people curiosities, it is time to work out another way to the same objectives, one which is more cautious, matter-of-fact and mundane. I have noticed, at bookstalls on railway stations, that Teresa of Avila, John of the Cross and *The Cloud of Unknowing* have become popular reading, as middle-class commuters try to spell out the spirituality they need for their suburban life, which is no longer as safe as it seemed.

It is possible that Hitler was a one-off affair; and it may be that the bomb will never be dropped (though the reverse seems a little more likely). When the world confronts darkness, an inner light becomes more necessary. It is the only light which can show what is mean and what is generous, and where integrity lies. It also (and this is no frivolous thought) shows us the joys that spirituality can provide in uncertain times. After all, political and economic revolutions outside us change very little unless there is a change and a revolution within us also.

My religious home is reform Judaism, but my

teacher told me long ago that a religious home need not be a religious prison. It was a good piece of advice. Like most people, I am attached to my religious centre by a cord which has plenty of stretch in it. It needs it because, like most people, I no longer live in a ghetto but am free-range. I wander, or am led, into other religious centres – especially Christian and Vedantist ones. Some things remain mysteries to any outsider, no matter how sympathetic, but a lot of spirituality can cross religious frontiers and be translated into other traditions, if we are careful and respectful. Whatever purists say, such translation is made every morning in religious broadcasts.

The secular world draws us together by the media, the bomb, pop culture and package holidays. It is important to spot the Holy Spirit, who can and does work through any and all of them.

I want to thank Mrs Daphne Richardson and Father Gordian Marshall, who made this selection. As in spirituality, seeing the obvious should be easy, but in practice it is difficult: it needs great discernment. They had this, and I am grateful and surprised (agreeably) by the result.

I have entitled the book *Day Trips to Eternity*, as I do not yet inhabit eternity. I visit it in moments; or, rather, it visits me. But I know it is home.

LIONEL BLUE

Falling in love

'Love makes the world go round', and the world hereafter too. Falling in love with God can be very similar to falling in love with a human being.

You bump into each other one day, or trip over each other. You meet at a boring formal occasion, like the wedding service of a distant relation – and suddenly you know you want to meet again. Or you realize with wonder that the old familiar God you met years ago in Sunday school classes is alive and attractive (not very different from the boy or girl next door in class B movies).

Or you start off by having values and find one day that they are alive. You can speak to them, they can answer back, and you can be in love with them as well as love them. They acquire a human face.

If you are hooked, you start haunting the place where you first met. You want to go to that particular church or synagogue and no other. It takes time to realize that God is everywhere.

Over and over again

I was going home in the London Underground late at night. Two young people sat opposite me, locked in an embrace which was as passionate as you can get when there is a seat-divider between you. As we clicked our way down the line, she told him he was beautiful and she loved him. He repeated it to her at the next station, and she lobbed the words back at him before we had scarcely moved. A woman in the carriage sighed, looked at them, and sighed again meaningfully at me.

I knew what she meant. It was repetitious and boring, and would never change. Somehow or other, those tired, hackneyed words would be as fresh to the lovers at the end of the line as they had been boring for us at its beginning. If you are inside the experience, such repetition is fresh; if you are outside the experience, all words are stale.

I thought of my prayers.

Risking the truth

Religion, real religion, begins when it can risk the truth. Conversion takes place when you can admit to yourself all the wrong reasons that are at work.

For many years I tried to pretend to myself, and my God became pretence too and the awareness of him make-believe. One day at a service, I said to myself, 'to hell with it!', recognized the impurity in myself, and knew that I was not God's boy-scout. At that moment, when I became myself and admitted what I was, I could pray.

At the time I thought my reasons for going into religion were important. Now I believe that, when I was brave enough to admit they were wrong reasons, I was right in applying. It sounds cock-eyed, but the truth digs deeper than our conventions.

Israel: 'One who struggles with God'

Judaism is a noisy religion. The faithful are rarely silent. Hosea said, 'Take with you words', and this commandment at least has been well kept. And as if their mouths are not enough, Jews also use their hands as they speak, argue and discuss. They do this with each other, and they do the same with God.

Jews even study divine law traditionally in pairs, so that they can argue better. How can one argue with oneself? Many feel uneasy with this vehement approach to religion. Surely God, they say, should be sought in silence, head reverently bowed, mind an inviting blank, eyes reverently closed. How can one seek the Divine in the atmosphere of a holy prize-fight?

Yet this is the meaning of the name Israel, 'one who struggles with God'. It was not given to Jacob after quiet meditation, but after prolonged and realistic struggle with a messenger of God; Jews, even in their religion, assert the humanness of humans; the arguing, contradictory, passionate side to our nature that God put in us. We are not holy vegetables, bits of religious asparagus, quietly growing upwards, complying with divine requirements, in a dull earthy silence.

Not *without* argument

It is important in our time that argument should continue inside the search for holiness, and be accepted within the tradition. Religious acceptance comes at the end, but one cannot cheat one's way there with a false passivity.

It is spontaneous, natural and right to protest at the suffering which falls on oneself or on another. So much of it seems unmerited, unhelpful and inconsequential. For a Jew it is not right just to endure persecution and concentration camps. He was given a mouth to ask, and limbs to act.

Only when protest and action have been tried, and the argument has been pursued to the deepest level, can he afford to give up with decency, and accept God's will with resignation.

No robot

It is sometimes forgotten how Jewish Jesus was in all his reactions. In the garden, he did not take the cup of suffering and bitterness without question. We do not know exactly what was said, and how much was expressed aloud, but we are left with a few significant words. 'Father, take this cup from me . . . nevertheless not as I will, but as thou wilt.'

There too is the sign of argument and struggle, for no Jew can ever be God's robot. He was not created to be a religious automaton, or a human prayer-wheel. He has to assimilate God's command into himself, and this means argument at the deepest level of his being.

Holy argument is the greatest path to God in Jewish experience, and dialectic is as effective for a Jew as a rosary is for a Catholic, in approaching the Almighty.

Bargaining with God

Abraham does not merely pray to God passively, begging the Almighty, he bargains with Him, arguing with the same intensity for the fate of the men of Sodom as any stall-holder in a Jewish market. The difference (and it is a very important one) is that he is not arguing for himself.

The argument never dries up. Balaam argues with his ass, Moses argues with the children of Israel, the children of Israel argue with each other, and with their Creator. He is, after all, their Father, not a stranger, and like all children they argue with Him. They cry from time to time that 'it's not fair'.

If there is intimacy and trust, such things can be done. It is much more natural, and more pious than putting God under a theological microscope, dissecting Him like a demonstration guinea-pig, with a detachment which is remote from the free play and intimacy of real love.

With all your wealth

'You shall love the Lord your God, with all your heart, and with all your soul, and with all your might', says the great Jewish prayer which comes from Moses himself. Heart and soul, oddly enough, presented little problem to the commentators. They had more difficulties with the word 'might'.

One interpretation was that it meant all one's bodily strength. The interpretation that hit home, however, and which was implemented in daily Jewish life, was that it meant 'money', that is, that we should love God with all our money and our wealth. Such is the holy materialism of Judaism.

Our ancestors brought sheep and goats and bullocks to God, because these were their money, the hard currency of those times. We bring our earnings too. Is there anything better? Do words, or thoughts, or dreams have more value?

God our Employer

Every religious person tries to describe his relationship to God, the link which connects him to the unseen source of power.

Although God is our Father, in daily life it is often better to think of him as our Employer. According to the Jewish commentaries and readings of the Torah, the children of Israel firmly state what is the best terminology for their religious purpose. 'Do not call us your children,' they cry, 'call us your builders!' Jews describe themselves as 'employees', and God as the 'Employer'.

They go even further. They use language which is as daring in its way as the language about the Body of Christ for a Christian. They talk about themselves as 'co-partners with God, in the work of creation'.

The details of all this are spelt out and they need no apology or gloss. God is 'faithful to pay our wages', says the Talmud. And it adds: 'the interest on good deeds can be enjoyed in this world' and – wonder of wonders – 'the capital remains intact for us in the world to come'.

Patching up the world

Jews try to earn their way to heaven, by patching up the world, and making it work. They have deliberately chosen religious prose, not because they could not write religious poetry, but because this was their service and their sacrifice.

It is said that 'the lion shall lie down with the lamb'. Since Jews do not expect miracles, or pray for a change in the instincts of lions or lambs, it is a matter which requires thought and organization. Someone, says one of the traditional commentators, will have to put a fence between them, and that someone will probably be a scribe or a Pharisee.

It was all summed up, long ago, by a contemporary of Jesus. Rabbi Tarphon says, 'The day is short, the work is great, and the labourers are sluggish, and the wages are high, and the Master of the house is insistent. It is not your duty to *finish* the work, but you are not free to neglect it.'

The job in hand

Which work is higher, which work is lower? Who
knows! Each one of us is given his own work, and
until we have done it, this is the highest for us.

The laws of the Torah are not the most ethereal,
nor the most poetical, but they are the ones God
has set for his people.

Which is more needed, earthly love or mystical
love? The former at least makes the world go
round, and ensures that mystics are born!

Earning our living

The material world we live in is not only the place of our work, it is the material we work with. No artist, no craftsman, can despise his own tools, and the medium he works in.

No Jew can ever really deplore or despise the world. It can irritate him and hurt him, but he cannot reject it. Even wanting to do so would be irreligious. It is where God put us, where we have to earn our living.

When we have done this, but not before, we can turn to other realities, and worlds which certainly exist. Until then, it is better not to dwell on them, except as compass points for finding our way.

They are the joys of a religious retirement, which most of us have yet to earn. In the meantime we get on with the job.

Being ordinary

Being very ordinary, most Jews have no wish to be great saints, great sufferers or indeed great anything. They have no wish to live on the edge of madness or inspiration and they turn to their religion to help them live ordinary lives in an extraordinary situation.

Religion is not there to intensify the emotions, it is there to make them usable and livable with day by day. Anti-semitism, prejudice, refugees, states of emergency and persecution are not experiences of a moment, they are facts to be lived with, all one's life.

The synagogue, the Law and the myriad details of Jewish custom are not there to provide an extra-ordinary experience; they are there to stabilize it, analyse it and cut it down to size. The chosenness and peculiarity of Jewish history are odd enough in themselves, they need no underlining.

'Holy impertinence'

A Jew does not pray primarily to ask for things, nor to have an experience, nor even to feel God's grace; he prays as he does his other tasks, to do his duty, and restate the facts and truths of existence with regularity.

The Hebrew word for prayer has little to do with the 'praying' or 'begging' or 'asking' of other traditions. It is not an attempt to persuade or nag the universe to go off course, for the sake of our desires. Private prayers are said by Jews within and without the service. According to one rabbi, prayers of petition were 'holy impertinence' and 'assaults on heaven'.

Judaism is the wine of its people, it gives them their lift, but it is not their opium with its fantasy images.

The insecurities of Jewish life, and its precarious comforts, have forced on Jews a healthy respect for what is. 'Truth is our King', says the Prayer Book in every service. Religion is not the construction of the world we should like, but a way to know and accept the reality in which God has placed us.

Giving without strings

Is it necessary to experience God in order to work for him? For most people the answer is an emphatic yes, especially if the work is prayer. For Jews it is not quite so certain. We were not put into the world to experience his presence.

The synagogue service is shaped by the older service of the Temple, and prayers take the place of the old sacrifices. When a man saw the flesh of his animal burning, he saw his capital literally going up in smoke. The forms of sacrifice may be primitive, but their meaning is not – because it is a giving, not a taking.

Synagogue prayers which substitute for them have this same characteristic. There is pleasure in religion, but it comes from giving, and the greatest pleasure is giving without strings.

An extra dinner guest

We ask God in prayers to restore his presence to us – but most of us doubt whether his presence would be congenial company.

If the *Shechinah* (the Divine Presence) sat next to us at table, would we enjoy our dinner more or less? Our instinctive reaction is immediately 'less'.

The joy of God, the bliss, the warmth, the love have been so poisoned by hidden guilt (most of it unjustified) and evasion (mostly justified) that we cannot worship God because we have given him the attributes of a fiend. Only thus can we explain why suggestions about prayer, meditation and retreats call up such defensiveness.

Standing or kneeling

Christians and Jews are taught the same virtues, but by very different means. A Jew seeks humility, not by falling on his knees but by self-deflation in a joke; soul-searching is similarly replaced by alienation. He sees himself with ironic detachment, reflected in many cultural mirrors, and the result is not dissimilar.

This objectivity and detachment of religion also affects the way Jews approach things which lie at the heart of religion. God is not dependent on their feelings, and a gulf separates them.

This distance helps Jews to view the workings of the Almighty with a certain clarity, and acceptance. It is not assumed that he has arranged the cosmos to fit in with personal demands or that the power of creation can fit into a human image.

In prayer, Jews stand upright, facing God. They have their own position, and standing. The distance, which at first seems chilling, enables Jews to be themselves, and the Almighty to be himself as well. The distance is necessary for freedom so that they do not suffocate each other.

Learning the language

The language of prayer is learned like any other language: by effort, application and practice. But underneath all these is the question, 'Do we want this inner conversation?' If we want it enough, we will get it. The answer is in the will.

Now it does have a disconcerting side, it is true, but prayer has its own technology, so to speak, its own rules. One of them is consistent application.

It is not difficult to produce a mystical moment. The difficulty lies in recognizing it and keeping it, and persevering through non-mystical hours, days or years.

Here we come into the world of organization and habit. We have a cycle of weekly public readings in the synagogue. Can we have a cycle of daily private readings for our members? One which helps people to discover God in their daily life, in their anxieties of the morning, in their newspaper, their work and their loving.

The other voice

If there is any reality in prayer, it means that you are not the only one involved. You may be searching for God, but this would not help you if he were not searching for you, for the distance is immense, beyond the intellect and the imagination. A hand comes down from heaven, so to speak. Prayer makes us ready to grasp it and trust its strength.

One of the consolations of religion is precisely this – that we are not alone. I found it inconvenient, this other voice inside me, separate from my own, and it gave my conduct an erratic quality. Gradually over the years the two have learnt to live together. Occasionally the two voices even fuse, and this is a great bliss though a rare one. But since I accepted it, I have never felt alone.

Once again this individual experience is also a communal one. Because Judaism trusted in the unseen and what was not there, it survived. Those who trusted in something more real have not.

Sharing the kitchen

Sooner or later the crisis will come, and you will have to take Him (or Her) back to your place. It is difficult because the Holy One does not fit your furniture or your books. If you are a Jew you will have to rearrange your kitchen, for example. As in any love affair you will have to make room for Him inside yourself as well, in your heart.

It is not easy sharing a kitchen with anybody, and it is even less easy sharing yourself with another being. After the first rapture, there is the adjustment period when you both have to learn to live together. It can be very irritating.

He wants to pray and you want to go sailing. You would like a ham rasher or a battery chicken, and He says He could not stand it.

If the love and commitment are strong you can overcome the gap, and like many couples you will gradually become more alike, and one day you may fuse together.

Signs of reality

If I had not trusted the signs, those hints of a greater reality, I would certainly have ceased to grow. I would have shrivelled. They have been and still are my only protection against being hijacked by society or my own ego.

I have seen good people who did not follow their own signs and became reflections of the media or of success. They began to lose their souls, and I did not want it to happen to me.

I use this awareness of a greater reality as a touch-stone. I hold things up to it: my feelings, my ambitions and my fantasies. It illuminates them, and I know what I must put aside and what I can keep. I rarely want to thank it – most liturgy, I think, overdoes this – it needs to be used not complimented.

The only things I ask of it with reasonable confidence are the knowledge of what I should do next or the perception of what is really going on – in me and around me. I suppose if I had greater trust I should ask more, but modesty and common sense restrain me. I cannot ask more than I believe.

The transformation

I should like to stress that with the awareness of God, the world does not vanish, it is the same world as before, the world which is seen by everyone. Nevertheless, in the light of this awareness, a transformation does take place.

Things which seemed important fade into shadows and insignificance. Dark areas light up, and incidents which were small or rejected begin to glow – and become the landmarks in my life.

It redefines success and failure, triumph and tragedy. With it I am released from the pull of my conditioning and can for a moment see clearly without the distortions of hope or fear.

It gives me courage to think my own thoughts, not packaged ones, and to walk one step alone, if I have to.

Unexpected effects

One of the most unexpected effects of prayer was for me the gift of laughter. Life seemed lighter, more buoyant. Perhaps it was because I trusted it a little more, did not fight it and could flow along with it.

Another unexpected side-effect was that I became more difficult to live with. This occurred especially after retreats. I suppose it was because I was working on two levels, and was, as a result, more inconsistent and more puzzling to others around me and to myself.

A moment of grace had come, but I just could not keep it, could not hold it, so I felt sad, for I had lost something. I could not acquire it or buy it, I had to wait for it in patience.

Totting up pious points

Humour is the great solvent which counteracts the rigidity to which Judaism is prone. When a religion concentrates on community and external acts as Judaism does, it is subject to definite diseases.

It is so concerned with doing, as opposed to being, that its assessment of spirituality becomes mathematical. Jews tend to tot up the number of commandments they have kept, and then look at everybody else's totals and compare results. In this pietistic game the one with the highest number wins.

Mechanistic piety is the price for spiritual objectivity. As the passion for detail turns into an obsession, the Jewish world is liable to compulsive neuroses. Rabbis and congregations chase after the ingredients of glue on postage stamps, the oil in sardine-tins, and kosher kiss-proof lipsticks.

Only humour and holy jokes save the Jewish world from the ridiculous. Heresy and fanaticism are the result of too logical minds, and humour is the best antidote.

Down to earth

Humour is not just an alleviation of pain, it also brings the infinite down to earth.

God has no human form in Jewish theology but he reveals a very human psyche in Jewish jokes. There he enters into the suffering and paradoxes of the world, and experiences the human condition.

There he is immanent, if not incarnate, and a gossamer bridge of laughter stretches over the void, linking creatures of flesh and blood to the endlessness of the Eternal and the paralysing power of the Lord of Hosts.

Under thirty feet of water

It was announced in Tel Aviv that God was going to send a tidal wave, thirty feet high, over the city because of its sins.

Muslims went to their mosques to pray for a speedy translation to the paradise of the prophet.

Christians went to their churches to pray for the intercession of the saints.

The Jews went to the synagogues and prayed, 'Lord God, it's going to be difficult living under thirty feet of water!'

More Martha than Mary

The aim of Jewish study was not really the knowledge of God. That was too daring. It was not expected that any beatific vision would come to the intellect, or that it would be possible to take degrees in religious experience.

Theology was not at the heart of religion, nor did the rabbis make the nineteenth-century mistake of equating piety with culture. The aim of Jewish study was not to experience God, but to know his will. The former is, after all, a pleasure, but the latter is duty and work.

Law, commandments, statutes, and ordinances are the daily bread of any society, holy or otherwise. Philosophy is the decoration.

As a religion Judaism was temperamentally closer to the attitudes of Martha than to those of Mary.

For its own sake . . .

The greatness of study came from the purification which accompanied it. It was this which made the argument and study holy. Without it, study becomes mere cleverness, and falls into the same traps as the modern Ph.D. industry.

The warning is contained in the earliest writings of the Talmud. Study of the Torah, it says, must not be used as a spade to dig with, nor as a crown to crown yourself with. It must be done for its own sake. Time and time again, through tractate after tractate, the words 'for its own sake' are used. This was the great defence against using religion for ambition and vanity – a dangerous mixture.

The lessons of this extend far beyond religion. The modern world is as preoccupied with argument and study as the rabbinic world, and there is a boom in cleverness.

Behind the masks

Truth seemed to come in many ways. There was
the inner truth of experience and feeling, and the
external truth of form and analysis. There was the
truth you discovered yourself, which became part
of you, and the truth you learnt from books,
which just adhered to you.

There were all the masks you had to wear during
a day. There was the mask you wore for your
boss, and the mask you wore for the person
beneath you, and the mask you wore for your
own protection or delight.

And behind all these masks, was there a real face,
or the image of God, or only another mask? I did
not know.

The 'real' person

In the Book of Leviticus there is the sentence, 'You shall love your neighbour as you love yourself'. There is a sharp rabbinical comment that this implies you must first love yourself before you can start trying out your love on others.

I had learnt this myself the hard way, before I ever read the commentary. But this led to another question: what was this self I was supposed to love?

Until my analysis, I had never dared to tackle this problem because I had never liked myself. Whether his theories were right or wrong, my analyst did like me and this gave me enough confidence to start. When I say he liked me, I mean the 'me' that actually existed, not the masks I wore – the bright boy, the good son, the committed Jew, or an addition to the baptismal font.

I have always been more interested in the analyst's commitment than in his theories or symbols. A bit of real fondness for the 'real' person goes a long way.

Holy places

What are the real holy places of a man's life? Where do his deepest experiences occur?

Is it in a 'place of worship', or in his place of business? Where does he ask the great religious questions? Perhaps it is when he lies awake on his bed. The Psalms certainly indicate this. Perhaps it is in the cafés; some, like Leah Goldberg, the Israeli poetess, see God in the smoke of cigarettes.

If one is going to make hierarchies of holy places, Jewish feeling would probably choose the home — for there the joy of holiness is most concentrated and most felt.

The synagogue, then, is not the highest or the holiest, but it is certainly the busiest centre of a man's life in religion, and it assumes that there is no life that is not in religion. God is present in one's life and in the world.

A synagogue, a holy place, does not make him present — it helps the worshipper or the student (there is little distinction between the two among Jews) to recognize it as being there.

The face of love

I had to work out if our love was exclusive or not. Did the love of God rule out the other loves of my life? Was he in fact jealous? With some people it does not seem that the relationship is like that.

I increasingly came to see him not as a rival to other loves but as part of them. I looked into someone else's face with love, and found him present. He in fact showed me what love looks like – its true face.

Spiritual orphans

Here is a point worth remembering. We know God in a similar way to the way we know other people. It is the methods of cognition and knowledge which are different. Prayer and, to a lesser extent, reason replace the senses. Otherwise our attachment to God does not differ very much from the way a child develops its attachment to parents.

Prayer is an inner conversation which renews our love and attachment to this great 'other' in our lives. If we do not renew it we become spiritual orphans, children who are rich but deprived, a state which increases anxiety.

Anxiety and a sense of loss, as any religious psychoanalyst will tell you, are hallmarks of our time, and ultimately connected with this loss of attachment to the 'other'.

A day tripper to the kingdom

When I was a student at Oxford I read the parables of the kingdom of heaven.

Walking down the street, chairing a meeting or smoking in bed, I found the kingdom of heaven occasionally opened to me.

I did not pray; I was in prayer. It was not something to strive for; it was something to accept.

I also stepped out of the kingdom just as surely and involuntarily as I had entered into it. I was not ready to live in it. I was still only a day tripper into it on a tourist's visa.

Just passing through

Decoration and grandeur are impermanent things. Wealth and security can be enjoyed but cannot be held.

Jews are a wandering people, not because of their own inclinations, but because of their religious history. Any group which journeys, which goes on a pilgrimage, be it a person or a church, may enjoy but must not get too attached to the landscape through which it passes.

Attachments can be formed to a style of service, to a culture in which one has settled, to patterns of religious leadership, to clothes, to beautiful things and even to well-loved absurdities.

Just because they do not last for ever, such things are not bad, as much 'spiritual' thinking implies. After all, we share the same finiteness.

Nor are passing things necessarily tragic, as the Greeks considered. The end of the journey does not invalidate the experience on the way.

A way to be normal

Spirituality means something different to a Christian and to a Jew because they live in different situations. God has set them different tasks, and they have different needs.

For a Christian, spirituality is a push upwards or a way inwards — an adventure of the soul, which journeys out into a dark night. For a Jew, spirituality is a way to be normal in the night of persecution and the darkness of continuous insecurity.

For a Christian, Jewish spirituality is always pedestrian. For a Jew, the Christian's path is fantastic.

Hurts come when people misunderstand each other because they are close, not when people are distant and never understand each other at all.

Transforming the world

The transformation of what exists is the aim of Christians and Jews. But they approach it in different ways.

A Christian starts by saving his soul, and ends by saving the world, provided he has not stopped at pietism and forgotten the world, but forged ahead to holiness.

The Jew tries to change the world, and finds he has to redeem himself in the process.

His progress, too, can be halted, and instead of journeying from righteousness to holiness, he can end up by being side-tracked into politics. This is his own Jewish form of evasion. Good works and ethical theories exist in their own right, they are not substitutes for self-awareness.

Changing ourselves

If the aim of Judaism is a change in the world, can we bypass the stumbling-blocks in ourselves? The disasters of Jewish history have shown us that this is a pipe-dream – dabblers in politics, please note!

We cannot change the world as the Torah commands unless we change ourselves, for we are the world too, and the work begins at home. If we do not see what is inside us, we will always project our inner ignorance on to the world around us, and falsify it consciously or unconsciously with our desires, our hopes and our fears. We will never have the detachment to see the Truth that is our King, and we won't want to see it either.

It is more interesting to change others (for their own good, of course) than to give ourselves an honest look.

Selling courage

Religion certainly won't get us out of problems. Just look at the lives of the people who have tried to serve God: the prophets, the great rabbis, the martyrs and the saintly. Many of them endured trouble and suffering with little enough to show for their pains.

Religion does not get us out of our problems but it does help us to face them. It won't wish them away but it will show us what they really are. It may not give us comfort, but it will satisfy. It may not give us short-term success in the eyes of man, but it will give us integrity in the eyes of God, or our own self-respect. It will help us to see the nature, the flavour, of good and evil without needing an external ideology or person to confirm the obvious.

The presence of God is not our air-raid shelter, but our launching-pad into the unknown and the dark. In our religious organizations we are God's commercial travellers. We do not sell insurance but courage, the courage to face reality and deal with it in honesty.

Prisoners of hope

Jews do not have any illusion as to the balance of pleasure and pain in human life. On the contrary, Judaism assumes that there is a considerable amount of the latter. In fact, there is so much of it from the outside, that the task of religion is not to increase it by adding internal sufferings.

The task of religion is to reduce the preoccupation with suffering, in order that the people may remain sane, and keep their balance. The greatness of Judaism does not lie in transcending suffering, but in reducing it to proportion.

From experience, Judaism ought to put a cross at the centre of its faith. It does not, because this would mean a distortion of its task, which is to build God's kingdom in a chaotic world, and be his prisoners of hope.

Taking the plunge

Organized Religion is not religion itself, but it is a powerful stimulant to it. If you do decide to go into it, it is better to dive right in than to wander round the edges of the pool, putting in a toe and complaining that the water is too cold.

If you are a professional, the choice becomes clear and stark quite quickly. Are you doing what is right or what is expedient? Are you preaching what is fashionable or what is true? Are you more frightened of God or of your employers?

I like Organized Religion. It does not solve any religious problem by itself, but you are forced to get to the point of the problem quicker without wasting so much time.

I also need inner religion more, to help me see the obvious. If you are a rabbi, you can end up thinking that the whole world is the Jewish problem. You need God to see Palestinian refugees, the mixed marriages, the sexual and economic minorities and all the outsiders in an insider's world.

Religious fancy dress

Religious fancy dress is easy to buy, and the phoney and the genuine both exist in traditional and progressive uniform. Fortunately, there are still good tests:

1 That though it does not reject popularity, it does not make it the first priority.

2 That it aims at the awareness of the individual, not the tribalism of the group.

3 That it increases the sensitivity and feeling of people for each other, but does not help them to manipulate each other.

4 That as well as building external structures, it builds invisible temples inside us.

Letting go

Religious knowledge is unlike any other, in that it forces us to choose and change. It does not allow us to stand still.

If we reject its truth, we are left with a ruined game, and expelled from Eden. If we accept it, then we have to allow ourselves to be changed.

I put it this way to emphasize that the centre of change is in our will; we do not change ourselves, we allow something to change us. We are not in charge and therefore it is frightening.

Like any act of love, physical or emotional, prayer and awareness require an ability to let go, trust and accept. And the most difficult thing in the world is to let go. For however we may complain about the present, change and letting go of this type are not immediately welcome, although for many of us there is not much to lose.

Perhaps, as Marx says, we have nothing to lose but our chains, but we are accustomed to these chains of habit and they have become cosy.

The quality of silence

One Thursday, I passed a Quaker meeting-house when a meeting was about to take place. It was not for undergraduates who came on a Sunday but for Quaker farmers in the country round about.

I walked in, sat down, and was sucked into the silence. It is the only mystery the Quakers possess, but it is a very powerful one. Some people got up from time to time and said the normal things, reminding the Almighty of the more distressing current events as if he did not know them.

I did not bother about them. I wanted to go deeper into that silence, because I knew that something was in it. It was the same silence I had felt in synagogue after my Bar Mitzvah. I had picked up an old thread, and I was jolly well going to follow it and unravel it.

I attended that meeting every week for about two months, and the silence became deeper and more profound. It began to have a face, a personality and a voice.

A composite guru

Like many people, I wanted at first to find one system or one guru who had the answers to all my problems. I met quite a few who had the answers, but they were the wrong ones.

Reluctantly I decided that such a creature was not to be found. Reality was too complex to fit one system or one person. Each of us had a part of the answer, and out of the fragments I had to construct my own composite guru. There are a lot of cracks, and I prefer them to show. I do not trust people who 'know' too much and have more awareness of God than they have of their own limitations.

I constructed my composite guru, as I have said, while thumbing through paperbacks at airports or sitting in a train careering through Europe at night. My theology, such as it is, was worked out on the move. It is quite appropriate, for I have always felt a visitor in the world – it is my habitation but not my home.

Rediscovering love

I began to wander into church crypts at odd hours of the day on the off-chance that something might happen. I suppose it was meditation, but it seemed like conversation. Then the effects of it began. Something very odd occurred, and it set me back on my heels. Despite the stillness of it all, I rediscovered love. I had lost the power to love in my childhood, and now it had come back.

I did not give a hoot who Jesus was, but the parables of the kingdom hit me with their off-beat truth, like hammer blows. I was in a bus and the people ceased to be human cattle on their way to work, but souls on their way to eternity. I suddenly found the delight you can get from giving things up. Jesus and the saints invaded my prayer life, and I saw the world transformed.

Every lover sees it that way, but I did not realize I was in love. I still thought that to love you needed sex and a human being. They help, but are not necessary and can get in the way.

Not by cake alone . . .

Christian piety is worrying to many Jews, precisely because it is so attractive. But it seems too religious to be Jewish. There is more cake than daily bread in the diet, and a Jew gets worried by spiritual indigestion.

It is heady stuff, for the pupils of scribes and Pharisees. It is easy to get drunk on it, if one is not used to it, and if we get drunk how can we do our duty, and deal with the details of life – the fences, the quarrels and the committees which we were sent to sanctify?

For Jews, religious experience can lead away from the religious duty to which God called us, and for which he gave us so many laws and commandments.

Angels by gaslight

My grandmother (*bubbe*) took me on expeditions. On Thursday nights she woke me up and at dead of night, when the gas-lamps were turned down to a flicker, we went round the block, putting little packets through letter-boxes.

They were little parcels of money and food to help poorer families celebrate the coming Sabbath. They were given at night so that giver and receiver would never meet, and neither would feel obligation or shame. Occasionally we met other *bubbes* wrapped in shawls and shadows, waddling from house to house.

I was surprised when I first saw a picture of angels after I became an evacuee. Who could believe in their too sweet smiles, the peroxide blonde hair and the fairy wings? My angels were solid from the neck down. They were Semitic, rheumatic and waistless.

When the Messiah comes, they might levitate. In this reality their poor bodies were stuck only too closely to the earth.

Unlikely angels

In my life I have met many angels, and an unlikely lot they are.

An angel can be the first person you fall in love with, who lets you down gently and lightly and helps you go forward into the risks of light and love. You can hear one in a bus queue whose name you will never know, but who says something which answers some inner questions, some need which is barely understood. It can be that intimate and strange figure, one's guardian angel.

The analyst who came to my aid at a party was a messenger to me of deep significance. So was a charwoman; so was a Carmelite nun I only saw behind a grille. So was an East End horse.

Through a few creatures, human or animal, we are redeemed from our limitations and learn to meet what is strange and unfamiliar, and this is not quite natural – it is a little more, therefore it is supernatural.

A *childhood memory*

There is a memory from childhood which is the most difficult to tell, because I cannot even tell it to myself without feeling puzzled and foolish. Many years later in life I started to paint. Whatever picture I intended petered out, and I stopped being master of my own paint-brushes. They began to lead me instead.

On the canvas an East End street appeared. It was about four o'clock in the afternoon. The fading light was late autumn or early spring. The street was a quiet one with some disused stables. A child was there – that was me – and facing him at the other end of the street was another figure. It was not an ordinary person and it was not a pixie, gnome, fairy or Santa Claus either.

It was real and profound; peace and love flowed from it, and knowledge too. I had wondered about death, though it was distant. The figure absorbed it. On the canvas the figure tries to shine, but my technique is not good enough . . .

Renewing the meeting

I am sure there was some meeting, but I do not know what. A Christian I know, who saw the painting, told me it was Jesus; and a Jungian I know told me it was an archetype. As a Freudian Jew I am less specific.

But when I began to pray, many years later, I felt I was resuming a meeting or conversation that had been broken off long ago. I knew who was at the other end of the line because we had met before.

I used to make light of it but now I take it according to its own feeling, which is not light.

The kitchen altar

To understand my *bubbe*'s (grandmother's) kitchen, you must realize that it was a chapel and a vestry. She processed, there is no other word for it, to the living-room table which was our altar.

This is not the language of whimsy but the language of Jewish theology. For, on the table, among the pickles and herrings, were the great silver cup of wine, the bread waiting to be blessed and the candles for the sanctification of the Sabbath – all the things a Christian finds when he goes to church.

Airborne

Although it may seem odd, the experience of God is our extra bonus, our reward – it is the pleasure and joy of religion.

We trundle along the ground like planes about to take off. But, if we do not resist it, there is a mysterious upward thrust, and – good Lord! – we are airborne. This experience is the wine of religion, the joy which lies at its heart.

We search for God in our clumsy ways and, sometimes, we despair. But if we really search, a hand, as it were, comes down and pulls us up. We find to our surprise that we are not the only searchers. We are half-heartedly searching for God, but God is whole-heartedly searching for us.

This may seem a personal experience, some say disparagingly 'subjective'. But it is an experience witnessed again and again in the history of our people, by housewives and prophets, by rebbes and rabbis, by the ignorant and the learned, in every religious book of our history.

Getting carried away

Jewish problems do not centre on conversion, or conversion experience. That stage has been passed, whether we like it or not. By being born, we find ourselves on a moving train. God is the driver, and it is not easy to get off.

'Spirituality' for a Jew is his response to this situation, not his choice of it. This fact, this objectivity, makes us wear our spirituality (and its problems) with a difference. From the outset we are conscious of another will, greater than our own, whose power modifies our lives and our plans.

Religion is not our subjective experience, to be cultivated in order to be visible, but an objective fact. It is not something sought in the recesses of the human heart, it is only too clear in daily experience.

Jews, then, are normal people who got caught up in God's plan of salvation by a whirlwind. They have to live their lives as best they can, sandwiched between the force of the spirit and the resistance of the world. The journey has its thrilling moments, but the ride is neither comfortable nor cosy.

Without your consent

The vast majority of Jews never chose to be Jews, they were born into it. They did not choose God, God chose them, and there is not much they can do about it, even if they wanted to. This sense of destiny, of predestination almost, has been intensified by recent persecutions.

In the Middle Ages, baptism was a passport to freedom. The wonder is that so few people used it! There was no ceremony, however, which could change the blood in one's veins, or blot out one's ancestors. There was no act or confession which could take Jews off the train to the concentration camp. 'A Yid I was born, and a Yid I am', goes a folksong. This trite statement was good theology and painful reality.

For Jews, then, the major fact of their life has been decided without their having been consulted. Perhaps this is true for everybody, but for Jews it is conscious and obvious. This realization goes back very far into the Jewish past. It is stated quite brutally in the early Talmud: 'Without your consent you are born and without your consent you live and without your consent you die, and **without your consent you will have to give an account and a reckoning before the King above the King of Kings, the Holy One, blessed be He.'**

Cosmic supermarket

The world is like a corridor that leads to the door which is death. What is beyond it, is not dogmatically described. As one Pharisaic master reasonably said – no one has ever come back from there.

Yet at the entrance to Jewish cemeteries are the Hebrew letters which stand for 'the house of life'. Although there is no formal doctrine of purgatory, death certainly did not break the laws of causation, or reward and punishment.

It is typical of the Pharisees that they pictured the cosmos as a shop, a self-service store, in fact. Life was a kind of shopping expedition, with a party at the end. 'Everything is given on pledge, and a net is cast for all living. The shop is open, the shopkeeper gives credit, the account is open and the hand writes, and whoever wishes to borrow, may come and borrow, but the collectors go round every day, and exact payment from a man with his consent or without it, and their claims are justified, and the judgement is a judgement of truth. Yet everything is prepared for the feast!'

Light and darkness

In the Prayer Book is a sentence, repeated in every morning service. We are asked to bless God 'who forms light and creates darkness, who makes peace and creates all'. This is a deliberate and merciful misquotation of the prophet Isaiah, who could still pray to a God who was not only 'the maker of peace' but also 'the creator of evil'.

We may know this in our hearts, but we cannot say it aloud. Perhaps God was in the gas chambers of Auschwitz, for we know that the day of the Lord may be darkness, not light, but if we dwell on it, we may lose our reason and be incapable of doing our work.

The force of reality is so overwhelming that even Jews need some protection against it. Otherwise we, too, like poor van Gogh, may cut off our ears. Peace and harmony are desired by all men. Jews are not romantics but realists, and know that they cannot be purchased cheaply.

In God's light

I think that to see properly is to see religiously, because the real problem is not material but spiritual, and only in a religious light can we see the way ahead.

The light of God is honest, a generous light but not a flattering one. As it shines on the familiar world we know the world remains the same, but its appearance is changed. New areas which our hearts and minds could not encompass rise out of their darkness. Some shadows deepen, but the light is intenser too.

For an instant we see the world as we should, in its generosity and glow. It is the same world, indeed it is the real world, but we cannot keep it – just as our minds cannot rest in prayer.

We need this light to see the difference between the real and the phoney. In our time it is very subtle, but it is there. This is, in fact, the essence of the modern problem.

God for all seasons

The task of Judaism is to tie knots, uniting one reality with others beyond; making the kitchen pots and pans, the doorways to the life of eternity.

If Jewish life looks odd, filled with bizarre details and practices, it is because so many knots have been tied that the result may be a religious success, but it is certainly not an aesthetic one. But, after all, the meat in the butcher's shop, and the clothes we wear, reveal God as well as ethics and poetry. He is just as present in awkward, clumsy and ugly things as he is in the more obviously beautiful things, and in high-minded thoughts.

The will of God exists for divorce as well as for marriage, and we bless him in bad times as well as good (after all, what is the use of a good-time religion!).

He is not for Judaism, the God of buttercups and daisies, and poetic sunsets. His nature is found in the laws concerning martyrdom, and the cases where anger is permissible.

Beacons everywhere

The gates of the coming world are everywhere, if only one can see them.

When I first went sailing, well-meaning friends tried to show me buoys and beacons in the sea. I looked and saw nothing, while they saw beacons everywhere. As I did not know what to look for, I had no foretaste, no premonition of the sight. Therefore I could not see what all around me saw.

Then I saw the first one, and suddenly the sea opened out. Buoys, cones, flashing lights, appeared everywhere. The empty sea seemed as crowded as Piccadilly Circus.

So it is with Jewish life; every oddity, every departure from normal shows the tension, the effect in this world, when another which is far greater approaches it and disturbs it. It is like the disturbance in two heavenly bodies as they approach each other — marks on the smaller reveal the force which the larger exerts as it comes nearer.

These rules of Jewish Law, which seem so odd if we think of this world on its own, become understandable in relation to the existence of another world and another reality.

Sources and Index

The following abbreviations are used for the titles
of Rabbi Lionel Blue's writings:

BH *A Backdoor to Heaven* (Darton, Longman and Todd 1979)

GJP 'God and the Jewish Problem' in Dow Marmur (ed.), *A Genuine Search* (1979), quoted by permission of the Reform Synagogues of Great Britain

HSP *To Heaven with the Scribes and Pharisees* (Darton, Longman and Todd 1975; 1984)

TH *A Taste of Heaven* (Darton, Longman and Todd 1977)

The figures in bold type refer to pages of the
present book.

42	GJP 60–1	48	TH 47–8	55	HSP 66–7
43	GJP 49	49	BH 10–11	56	HSP 101
44	BH 29	50	BH 6–7	57	HSP 61–2
45	BH 112–13	51	BH 7	58	GJP 52
		52	TH 49	59	HSP 98
46	BH 30	53	GJP 43	60	HSP 98–9
47	HSP 21	54	HSP 67		